Book.

The N

MW01222790

Written by Susan Griffiths
Illustrated by Kerry Gemmill

Nelson

an International Thomson Publishing company I(T)P*

The
Night Crossing

With these characters ...

Aria

Aria's
Grandmother

Varga,
a Borgon!

"The Borgon

Setting the scene ...

The long, cold winter is coming, and with it, trouble. A brave young girl must save her village from starvation—or even worse, from a terrible battle that no-one will win.

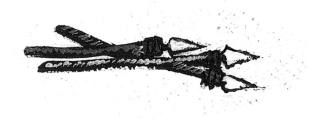

But before she can save her village, she must make a dangerous journey into enemy territory. She must travel through the dark forest, to where no-one has gone before: to the bleak village of her dreaded enemies, the Borgons.

e terrible, terrible creatures."

Chapter 1.

In the cold, dark forest, the old woman suddenly put her hand up as a warning. Her young companion stopped instantly, and their two donkeys, carrying heavy sacks on their backs, stood silently.

The old woman whispered the young girl's name.

"Aria?" she said. "Did you hear that?"

The young girl slowly moved forward and shook her head from side to side.

"I hear nothing, Grandmother," she replied softly. The four dark figures stood very, very still.

Finally, when the old woman was
certain there was no danger, they
moved on, carefully avoiding the twigs
that might snap under their feet.

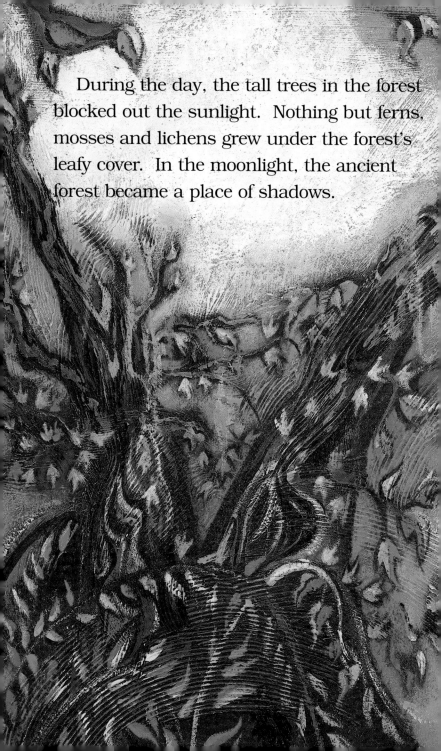

During the day, the tall trees in the forest blocked out the sunlight. Nothing but ferns, mosses and lichens grew under the forest's leafy cover. In the moonlight, the ancient forest became a place of shadows.

Aria and her grandmother could see nothing moving in front of them. But out of the sides of their eyes, they could catch a glimpse of shadows dancing and shifting. Without looking around, they felt like a hundred night creatures were approaching, all closing in.

Chapter 2.

Aria and her grandmother lived in an ancient village on the side of a deep valley. The villagers did not understand the shadows, or why the moon changed, or why the forest felt so scary at night. All they knew was that the darkest night, just before the winter, was the *only* safe night to walk through the forest. Only on that one night could you be sure that the dreaded Borgons would not come swooping down to capture you.

It was on this darkest night that the old woman and her granddaughter Aria guided their donkeys deeper and deeper into the forest, down the slippery slopes towards the river.

No-one in their village had seen a Borgon. Villagers told stories about them—stories about strange, evil half-people. The Borgons lived on the other side of the valley, where the sun never shone, and no vegetables or fruits grew. It was said they spoke a strange language that no-one could understand. Everyone in Aria's village was frightened of them. The Borgons in their stories were always very, very dangerous.

Although the villagers feared the Borgons, they needed something that the Borgons made. The Borgons had knowledge of a huge, endless lake, far from the valley. They knew how to use the water from that mysterious lake to make something vital for their survival. Without the Borgons, Aria's village would not survive each year's freezing winter.

Chapter 3.

The night before her dark, dangerous journey into the valley, Aria's grandmother announced that she was going to take Aria with her. Aria knew that her grandmother went away once a year at the end of autumn. Her grandmother was always missing for several days. But until now, Aria had not understood why.

"Let me explain," began her grandmother. "This is a job that the women in our family have done for many, many years—my mother, her mother and her mother before that. Only *we* know the secret path through the forest."

Aria listened carefully, her eyes wide open.

"During the spring and summer, we have food," said her grandmother. "The earth gives us all we need to keep healthy and strong. But during the winter, the plants do not grow. We must store food for the winter. We need salt to preserve our food. Without salt, our food will rot and we will starve."

"The Borgons are terrible, terrible creatures. They are more dangerous than the poisonous spiders in the forest. But everything has a purpose. If we do not disturb the spiders, they build webs to catch and eat the insects that cause problems for us. The Borgons, too, have a purpose. They, and they alone, know where to find salt."

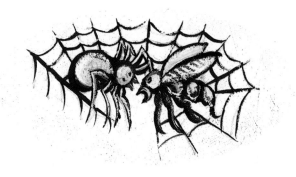

"On the darkest night before the winter, we must creep down to the edge of the river, and leave half of our store of vegetables on our side of the river. Then we must hide in the forest."

"During the night, the Borgons will cross the river and take the vegetables. In return, they leave us enough salt to preserve our food."

"After this trip, I will be too old to make this journey again. I must show you the secret path to the meeting place. Tomorrow night, you must come with me to the river's edge. We shall return with our winter's salt. I need your young eyes and ears to help me. The journey is never easy. Be ready for danger."

Chapter 4.

By the time Aria and her grandmother reached the river, the night was the blackest Aria could remember. Huge, dark clouds hid the few stars that were shining above the tree tops, and an icy wind blew along the valley. She shivered, half with cold, and half with fear.

"Here," called her grandmother. "Here, by this ancient gnarled tree, is where we lay our sacks of vegetables."

They left their sacks nestling amongst a tangle of roots. Aria could feel a hundred pairs of eyes on her, and was relieved when her grandmother waved her back into the forest.

"Now we sleep," she said. "We find the tallest tree, and we sleep in the branches, out of any danger."

"No Borgon will dare stay long on this side of the forest."

They tied up the weary donkeys in a small clearing away from the river. Aria helped her grandmother climb into the safety of the moss-covered branches. The winds blew stronger, and rain started to fall. By the time they fell asleep, a great storm was sweeping up the valley.

Unseen and unheard, shadows moved slowly out of the dark forest on the other side of the river. The shadows stepped silently into the rising river, looking and listening, and sniffing the night air. The Borgons were close. Very close.

Chapter 5.

As the storm raged on, the river rose higher. Very soon, the water was waist deep, and flowing fast. The Borgons were worried. It took three of them to carry the sack of salt across the river. They were exhausted.

"Varga," growled one of the Borgons. "Varga, we must go back before the river is too deep and we are trapped here." Varga turned and looked back at the rising river.

"Leave the salt at the ancient tree," he commanded. "It is too dangerous to carry the vegetables back now. We will return to get them as soon as we can."

The Borgons dropped their heavy load of salt, and struggled back into the raging river.

On both sides of the river, in two very tall trees, huddled two groups of cold sleeping figures. Through the valley the wind howled, and the water kept rising and rising.

Chapter 6.

When the sun rose, everything was calm again. Aria and her grandmother climbed down to the forest floor, and stared. All around were mud and piles of broken and twisted trees that had been swept down from far up the river.

"Let's get the salt," said Aria's grandmother. Aria could tell she didn't want to spend a moment longer in the forest. They picked their way over tree trunks, branches and through deep, black mud to reach the river bank. The ancient tree was one of the few left standing after the storm.

"There is no salt!" hissed the old woman angrily.

Aria searched around the tree trunk.

18

Her grandmother shook her fist at the forest on the other side of the river.

"And they have stolen our vegetables. Borgons!" She was furious.

When Aria and her grandmother returned to their village the next night, they told the villagers how the Borgons had tricked them. Not only were the villagers angry—they were very worried. With only a few weeks left before the winter snows, they had nothing to preserve their food with. Without the salt, all the vegetables would rot.

The villagers decided they would go to the Borgons' village and demand their share of the salt. They knew the Borgons were dangerous, so they prepared for a battle. They sharpened their spears, tightened their bows and made arrows out of reeds.

Aria sat by the fireside. She watched the villagers shouting out, "War! War! We will win the war against the Borgons!"

She was thinking. She did not want a war. Just as the Borgons had stolen their food, so she would quietly steal the salt from the Borgons' village.

When the villagers finally grew tired, and went to sleep, Aria crept away from her village. The forest seemed even blacker and more frightening than last night, but she was determined to follow the secret path to the river. Once there, she would cross and try to find the Borgons' own path. That would surely lead her to their village.

After an hour, the shadows in the forest were haunting Aria. She was cold and frightened, but carefully followed the path her grandmother had shown her, just a few nights ago.

The old trees seemed like ugly monsters, knotted and twisted with age. She saw shadows moving. Terrified, she turned around; and then there were more shadows moving behind her. She ran down and down, towards the river. She stopped, exhausted, panting for breath. Then the moon went behind a cloud, and the small silver and black shadows disappeared.

Aria breathed a sigh of relief. But at that moment, she saw a large black shape. Not to the side or behind her, but directly in front.

Chapter 7.

"Where are our vegetables?" demanded the Borgon, shaking Aria. "Why did you steal our salt and then take away the vegetables?"

Aria was in the Borgon village surrounded by large menacing figures. The walk from the river had been long and frightening for Aria. All around, the land was bare except for grey boulders and caves cut into the hillsides.

A tall, fierce-looking Borgon stepped into the middle of the circle and leaned down towards Aria.

"My name is Varga," he growled. "Without your vegetables, we will starve. Why did you do this? We left you the salt."

"We left *you* the vegetables!" said
Aria, confused. "You stole them and
left *us* no salt!"

Varga stared at Aria.
"There were no vegetables. We
returned the next day when the river
went down. There was nothing. You
had taken the salt *and* the vegetables!"

A wise old Borgon shuffled into the circle.

"It was some*thing* that took the food and the salt, not some*one*," he said in a fading breathless voice. Varga and Aria stared at the old Borgon, who was now sitting on a rock.

"What do you mean?" snapped Varga.

"It was the *river* that stole the vegetables and the salt," said the wise old Borgon. "The river is the thief that will make us *all* starve this winter."

Varga turned to Aria.

"We have only a little salt left," he said sadly. "It will not be enough to trade with your village for more vegetables."

Aria nodded sadly.

"We do not have enough vegetables to trade with you either," she said. "But without the salt, we will soon have none left at all."

24

The Borgons fell silent. Aria looked at them, and thought of her own village, worried about starving this winter.

"It will be a hard winter," she said. "But there is a way to survive—*together*."

Chapter 8.

The next day, the villagers couldn't find Aria anywhere. Aria's grandmother worried that she would never see her granddaughter again.

"The Borgons have stolen my granddaughter," she cried. "As if stealing our food was not bad enough!"

The villagers were furious. Aria's disappearance made them more determined to do battle with the Borgons.

Suddenly, the old woman heard a faint voice call. She couldn't believe her ears. She stood up, and squinted her eyes. There, at the edge of the forest, was Aria!

The villagers scurried down the hillside towards the edge of the forest. Aria smiled from the edge of the trees. She waved and started to run towards them. But the villagers' looks of joy turned to fear. Beside Aria, from behind a tree, stepped a *fierce, dangerous Borgon.*

The villagers drew back their bows as tight as they could and aimed directly at the Borgon beside Aria.

"Wait!" shouted Aria, holding up her arm. The villagers watched in horror as she whirled around and held her hand out to the Borgon. Varga moved slowly to her side. She held his hand and spoke loudly and clearly to the villagers.

"The Borgons did not steal our food. It was the raging river that washed it all away during the storm. Without each other, we *will* starve," called Aria. "But together, we can share what we have. We may make it through the long winter. But only if we share what is left."

Varga called to another Borgon, who walked slowly out of the forest. He carried a small sack of salt. He raised a handful and it shone in the sunshine. Aria's villagers lowered their weapons, still staring suspiciously at the two Borgons.

Aria's grandmother hobbled down the hillside, and put her arms around the young girl.

She knew it was going to be the longest, hardest winter that the village would remember. She knew that everyone would be hungry, with only half as much preserved food to eat. But she also knew that her granddaughter had made a very wise decision. She was proud of her. She knew that, from now on, the Borgons and the villagers could live together in peace.

Chapter 9.

Aria's grandmother turned to Varga, and for the first time in her life, stared fearlessly into the eyes of a Borgon. Then she reached out her hand. Varga reached out and took her hand. Then he surprised everyone by speaking in a language that was the same as their own.

"Together we share!" he said.

Simple, wise words that changed the valley forever.

Deep, dark forest, danger all around,
Food to leave and salt to be found.

Rain falls, wind blows,
Figures sleep, but trouble grows.

The river rises in winter grey,
It steals the food, sweeps the salt away.

No food for the Borgons! They will surely die.
No salt for the villagers—they will not survive!

Each blames the other and prepares for war,
The villagers are furious, the Borgons roar.

But one small girl, much smarter than the rest,
Goes alone to the forest (she knows what's best).

She meets the Borgons, shaking in fear,
Their salt, their food, maybe to share?

In talk and understanding, they both realise,
That each needs the other, they'll **together** survive.

Villagers not mean, Borgons not fierce,
Together united, both live in peace.